COOKING WITH HARISSA

DELICIOUS RECIPES WITH A SPICY NORTH AFRICAN STYLE

By
Umm Maryam
Copyright © 2015 by Saxonberg Associates
All rights reserved

Published by
BookSumo, a division of Saxonberg Associates
http://www.booksumo.com/

INTRODUCTION

Welcome to *Cooking with Harissa: Delicious Recipes with a Spicy North African Style*!

This cookbook is all about Harissa. Harissa is a North African chili paste that can you buy in stores. But of course homemade versions are always better.

We will start this cookbook learning two types of delicious harissa recipes, a classical version, and a great Tunisian style.

This harissa adventure will take us all throughout the African world and also the Asian world, with some Indian recipes, as well.

Harissa is great for stews, as a topping for meat before it is roasted, and even as a spread on toasted bread.

Cooking with unique ingredients like apricots, cinnamon, ginger, plums, and oils make great and memorable recipes. You find these unique ingredients used throughout the cookbook.

TABLE OF CONTENTS

Introduction 2

Table of Contents 3

Any Issues? Contact Me 8

Legal Notes 9

Common Abbreviations 10

    Homemade Harissa 11

    (Classical North African Style) 11

    Homemade Harissa 13

    (Classical Tunisian Style) 13

    Plums, Tomatoes, and Samosas 15

    (Indian) 21

    Apricots and Lamb 25

(Moroccan) 25
Spinach Potatoes and Eggs 28
(Tunisian) 28
Sun Dried Tomatoes, Cinnamon, and Beef Puff Pastry 31
Chipotle Chicken Breast 34
Paprika Harissa Lemon Fish.. 37
Persian Couscous with Harissa and Currants 40
Kale and Sweet Potato Stew.. 42
Spicy Carrot Paste... 45
North African Pizza.. 47
Harissa Burgers 50
Moroccan Style Couscous 52
Orange Cinnamon Chicken 54
Harissa Shrimp and Coriander 56
Beet Salad 58
(Tunisian) 58
Spicy Cauliflower 60

Mushroom Kebabs 62
Classical Moroccan Tagine I 64
Vegan Zucchini 66
(Tunisian) 66
Beef Koftas 69
(Moroccan Style) 69
Harissa Ginger and Cinnamon Lamb 71
(Moroccan) 71
Potatoes from Tunisia 73
Spicy Garbanzo Dip 76
Pistachio and Fig Tagine 79
Countryside Beef 82
(Tunisia) 82
Harissa Pasta 85
Harissa Dump Dinner 88
Mediterranean Mango Salad 90
Lentils and Shrimp 92

Creamy Chicken Quarters 95
Orange and Pine Nut Fish 97
Shakshouka 99
(Spicy Poached Eggs in Tomato Sauce) 99
(Algerian) 99
North African Breakfast 102
Mediterranean Vegetarian Tagine 105
Classical Lentils 107
Balsamic Bake 110
Moroccan Parsnips 113
Coconut Ceviche 115
(Morocco) 115
North African Style Dip 118
Tomato Shrimp 120
Harissa Crab Bake 123
East African Penne 126
(Ethiopian) 126

Mediterranean Meatballs 129

Pumpkin Tagine 131

Cranberry Tagine 134

Mediterranean Lamb Sausage Burgers 136

Carrots, Harissa, Peppers, Chicken, and Sausage Couscous 138

THANKS FOR READING! NOW LET'S TRY SOME **SAMOSAS**, **BIRYANI**, AND **MOROCCAN** 141

Come On 143

Let's Be Friends :) 143

Can I Ask A Favour? 144

INTERESTED IN MY OTHER COOKBOOKS? 145

ANY ISSUES? CONTACT ME

If you find that something important to you is missing from this book please contact me at umm@booksumo.com.

I will try my best to re-publish a revised copy taking your feedback into consideration and let you know when the book has been revised with you in mind.

:)

— Umm Maryam

LEGAL NOTES

ALL RIGHTS RESERVED. NO PART OF THIS BOOK MAY BE REPRODUCED OR TRANSMITTED IN ANY FORM OR BY ANY MEANS. PHOTOCOPYING, POSTING ONLINE, AND / OR DIGITAL COPYING IS STRICTLY PROHIBITED UNLESS WRITTEN PERMISSION IS GRANTED BY THE BOOK'S PUBLISHING COMPANY. LIMITED USE OF THE BOOK'S TEXT IS PERMITTED FOR USE IN REVIEWS WRITTEN FOR THE PUBLIC AND/OR PUBLIC DOMAIN.

COMMON ABBREVIATIONS

cup(s)	C.
tablespoon	tbsp
teaspoon	tsp
ounce	oz
pound	lb

*All units used are standard American measurements

Homemade Harissa

(Classical North African Style)

Ingredients

- 6 oz. bird's eye chilies, seeded and stems removed
- 12 cloves garlic, peeled
- 1 tbsp coriander, ground
- 1 tbsp ground cumin
- 1 tbsp salt
- 1 tbsp dried mint
- 1/2 C. chopped fresh cilantro
- 1/2 C. olive oil

Directions

- Add the following to the bowl a food processor: chilies, cilantro, garlic, salt mint, coriander, and cumin.
- Pulse the mix until it is smooth then add in some olive oil and pulse the mix a few more times.
- Place the mix in jar and top everything with the rest of the oil.
- Enjoy.

Amount per serving (40 total)

Timing Information:

Preparation	
Cooking	20 m
Total Time	20 m

Nutritional Information:

Calories	28 kcal
Fat	2.8
Carbohydrates	0.9g
Protein	0.2 g
Cholesterol	0 m
Sodium	176 m

* Percent Daily Values are based on a 2,000 calorie diet.

Homemade Harissa
(Classical Tunisian Style)

Ingredients

- 11 oz. dried red chile peppers, stems removed, seeds, removed
- 3/4 C. chopped garlic
- 2 C. caraway seed
- 1/2 tsp ground coriander seed
- 2 tsps salt

Directions

- Let your chilies sit submerged in water for 30 mins then remove the liquids.
- Now add the following to the bowl of a food processor: salt, pepper, coriander, garlic, and caraway.
- Puree the mix then place everything into a Mason jar and top the mix with a bit of oil.
- Place the lid on the jar tightly and put everything in the fridge.
- Enjoy.

Amount per serving (192 total)

Timing Information:

Preparation	
Cooking	40 m
Total Time	1 h

Nutritional Information:

Calories	10 kcal
Fat	0.3 g
Carbohydrates	1.9g
Protein	0.4 g
Cholesterol	0 m
Sodium	26 m

* Percent Daily Values are based on a 2,000 calorie diet.

Winter Tagine

Ingredients

- 2 tbsps olive oil
- 1/2 onion, diced
- 1 (15 oz.) cans chickpeas, drained & rinsed
- 1 (15 oz.) cans diced tomatoes
- 1 tbsp fresh Italian parsley, minced
- 1 tbsp fresh cilantro, minced
- 1/4 tsp salt
- 1/4 tsp black pepper
- 1/4 tsp harissa
- 1/4 tsp cinnamon
- 1/4 tsp turmeric
- 1/4 tsp ginger
- 1/4 tsp cumin

Directions

- Stir fry your onions in oil for 7 mins then add in: cumin, ginger, turmeric, cinnamon, harissa, black pepper, salt, cilantro, and parsley.
- Stir the spices into the onions and cook everything for 60 more secs.
- Now add the diced tomatoes and chickpeas.
- Stir the mix again then place a lid on the pot and cook everything for 35 mins with a low level of heat.
- Enjoy.

Servings: 2

Timing Information:

Preparation	5 mins
Total Time	35 mins

Nutritional Information:

Calories	426.6
Cholesterol	0.0mg
Sodium	940.4mg
Carbohydrates	59.9g
Protein	12.9g

* Percent Daily Values are based on a 2,000 calorie diet.

Honey, Harissa, and Eggplants Tagine

Ingredients

- 2 tbsps olive oil
- 1 tsp cardamom seed
- 1 cinnamon stick
- 1 large onion, diced
- 1 large eggplant, diced
- 2 garlic cloves, crushed
- 2 tbsps harissa
- 1 can diced tomatoes
- 1/2 C. vegetable stock
- 2 tbsps honey, plus
- extra honey, to drizzle
- 2 tbsps of fresh mint, diced

Directions

- Fry your cinnamon and cardamom in oil for 1 mins then add in the eggplants and onions.
- Continue to fry everything for 5 more mins then combine in the stock, garlic, tomatoes, and harissa.
- Let everything simmer for 12 mins then add some pepper, salt, and the honey.
- Stir in the honey and spices then shut the heat.
- When serving the tagine top each serving with more honey and some mint.
- Enjoy.

Servings: 4

Timing Information:

Preparation	10 mins
Total Time	25 mins

Nutritional Information:

Calories	187.3
Cholesterol	0.0mg
Sodium	12.0mg
Carbohydrates	30.5g
Protein	3.7g

* Percent Daily Values are based on a 2,000 calorie diet.

Plums, Tomatoes, and Samosas (Indian)

Ingredients

- 2 tbsps pine nuts
- 2 C. coarsely chopped plums
- 2 tbsps shallots, chopped
- 1 1/2 tsps olive oil
- 1 1/2 tsps butter
- 2 medium tomatoes, quartered
- 1 garlic clove, chopped
- 1 tbsp sugar
- 1/2 tsp harissa
- 1 thyme, sprig
- 1 vanilla bean
- 1/2 tsp chopped fresh basil
- 1/4 tsp salt
- cooking spray
- 1/2 C. thinly sliced yellow onion
- 1 lb Yukon gold potato, peeled and cut into 1/4-inch cubes
- 1/2 C. carrot, chopped
- 2 1/2 tsps red curry paste
- 1 garlic clove, diced
- 1 C. water
- 1/3 C. light coconut milk
- 2 tsps fresh lime juice
- 1/4 tsp salt
- 1 tsp ground turmeric
- 1/2 tsp ground ginger
- 1/2 tsp ground cinnamon
- 6 3/4 oz. all-purpose flour
- 1/2 tsp salt
- 1/4 tsp baking soda
- 1/4 C. hot water
- 6 tbsps fresh lemon juice
- 7 tsps peanut oil, divided

Directions

- Begin by toasting your pine nuts for 3 mins with no oil in a large pot, then add in the garlic, plums, tomatoes, shallots, butter, and olive oil.
- Get the mixing gently boiling, then set the heat to low, and continue to simmer the mix for 35 mins. Stir the mix every 5 mins.
- Now combine in: the vanilla bean, sugar, thyme, and harissa.
- Stir the mix and continue cooking everything for 25 more mins.
- Now shut the heat, place a lid on the pot, and let the contents sit for 40 mins.
- Take out the vanilla and thyme and throw them away. Then add in 1/4 tsp of salt and the basil. Stir the mix.
- Get a frying pan hot with nonstick spray then begin to fry your potatoes and onions for 7 mins, set the heat to low, and stir in the garlic, curry paste, and carrots.
- Continue to cook the carrots for 7 mins while mixing everything.
- Combine in the coconut milk and 1 C. of water and get the mix boiling.
- Once the mix is boiling set the heat to low, and continue to simmer everything for 17 mins until most of the moisture has cooked out.
- Now combine in 1/4 tsp of salt and the lime juice.
- Stir the mix then place everything into a bowl.
- Let the potatoes lose their heat then mash everything together.
- Get a separate frying pan and begin to toast your cinnamon, turmeric and ginger in it for 1 min then remove the spices to the side.
- Now add the following to the bowl of a food processor: baking soda, flour, 1/2 tsp salt, and toasted cinnamon mix.

- Process the mix a bit to evenly combine it then add in the following: 1 tbsp peanut oil, 1/4 C. hot water, and lemon juice.
- Process the mix again until you have a dough.
- Get a bowl and coat it with nonstick spray and place the dough in the bowl.
- Place a damp kitchen towel over the bowl and let it sit for 20 mins.
- Now break your dough into twelve pieces and flatten each into a circle.
- In the middle of each circle add 2 tbsps of the potato mix. Coat the outside of each piece of dough with some water and shape everything into a semi-circle and seal each, with a fork.
- Do this for all your dough and potato mix.
- Now begin to fry half of the samosas in 2 tsp of hot peanut oil for 5 mins.
- Flip each one and continue frying them for 4 more mins.
- Now fry the rest of the samosas in an additional 2 tsp of oil for the same amount of time.
- Top the samosas, with the harissa mix, when serving them.
- Enjoy.

Amount per serving: 1

Timing Information:

Preparation	2 h
Total Time	4 h

Nutritional Information:

Calories	163.5 g
Cholesterol	1.2mg
Sodium	230.6mg
Carbohydrates	27.5g
Protein	3.1

* Percent Daily Values are based on a 2,000 calorie diet.

Apricots and Lamb

(Moroccan)

Ingredients

- 2 tbsps extra-virgin olive oil
- 1 tsp cumin seeds
- 1 onion, thinly sliced
- 4 cloves garlic, crushed
- 1 sweet potato, peeled and diced
- 2 (1 lb) lamb shanks
- 1 (14.4 oz.) can chopped canned tomatoes
- 1 1/4 C. chopped dried apricots
- 1 1/2 tsps harissa
- salt and pepper to taste
- 2 tbsps slivered almonds
- 1 C. quick-cooking couscous
- 2 tbsps extra-virgin olive oil

Directions

- Stir fry your cumin seeds in 2 tbsp of olive oil for 60 secs then add in the sweet potatoes, onions, and garlic.
- Set the heat to low and place a lid on the pot.
- Leave the potatoes for 7 mins and try to stir them at least twice as they cook.
- Place your lamb into the pot and brown the meat all over for about 10 mins then combine in the harissa, tomatoes, and apricots.
- Stir the mix then combine in some pepper and salt. Add a bit more water and get everything boiling.

- Once the mix is boiling, place a lid on the pot, set the heat to low, and cook the mix for 60 mins.
- Stir every 10 mins.
- In a separate pan begin to toast your almonds for 7 mins, with no oil, then place them to the side.
- Get a bowl and add in your couscous. Combine the warm water with the couscous and let everything sit for 7 mins.
- Combine the almonds and 2 tbsps of olive oil with the couscous and place everything into a platter.
- Top the couscous with the lamb, its drippings, and the veggie fruit mix in the pan.
- Enjoy.

Amount per serving (2 total)

Timing Information:

Preparation	10
Cooking	1 h 30 m
Total Time	2 h

Nutritional Information:

Calories	1256 kcal
Fat	54.5 g
Carbohydrates	121.4 mg
Protein	70 g
Cholesterol	179 m
Sodium	824 m

* Percent Daily Values are based on a 2,000 calorie diet.

Spinach Potatoes and Eggs (Tunisian)

Ingredients

- 1/3 C. vegetable oil
- 2 potatoes, peeled and cubed
- 8 oz. diced chicken breast meat
- 1 large onion, diced
- 1 tbsp harissa
- 1 1/2 tsps ras el hanout
- 1/2 C. water
- 1 1/2 tbsps tomato sauce
- 1 tbsp butter
- 1 bunch fresh spinach, washed and chopped
- 8 eggs
- 1 C. frozen peas
- 1/3 C. Parmesan cheese
- 1 pinch salt and pepper to taste

Directions

- Coat a casserole dish with nonstick spray then set your oven to 400 degrees before doing anything else.
- Fry your potatoes in veggie oil for 10 mins then place them to the side.
- Add in the rest of the oil and begin to fry your chicken in it for 3 mins then combine in the onions.
- Keep cooking everything for 7 mins then combine in the butter, harissa, tomato sauce, ras el hanout, and water.

- Stir the mix until it is all evenly combined, then get everything boiling.
- Once the mix is boiling, set the heat to low and place the spinach in.
- Once the spinach is soft shut the heat and place a lid on the pot.
- Get a bowl and whisk your eggs in it then combine in the potatoes, parmesan, and peas.
- Combine this mix with the chicken mix and top everything with some pepper and salt and place the mix into the casserole dish.
- Cook everything in the oven for 25 mins.
- Enjoy.

Amount per serving (12 total)

Timing Information:

Preparation	30 m
Cooking	35 m
Total Time	1 h 30 m

Nutritional Information:

Calories	193 kcal
Fat	11.7
Carbohydrates	11.4
Protein	11.4
Cholesterol	139 m
Sodium	157 m

* Percent Daily Values are based on a 2,000 calorie diet.

Sun Dried Tomatoes, Cinnamon, and Beef Puff Pastry

Ingredients

- 1 onion, cut into 6 pieces
- 1 onion, diced
- 3 lbs beef stewing beef, cut into 3 cm cubes
- 2 tbsps harissa
- 2 tbsps plain flour
- 140 g tomato paste
- 1 C. dry red wine
- 2 C. beef stock
- 2 bay leaves
- 1 cinnamon stick
- 1 C. pitted kalamata olive
- 1/2 C. sun-dried tomato
- 1/4 C. of fresh mint
- 6 sheets frozen butter puff pastry, thawed before using
- 1/4 C. lightly packed brown sugar
- 1 egg, beaten

Directions

- Set your oven to 325 degrees before doing anything else.
- Get a bowl, combine: the harissa and beef.
- Evenly coat the pieces of beef.
- Now brown the beef all over, in oil, in a skillet, then add in the onion and continue frying everything for 5 mins.
- Combine in the tomato paste and cook the mix for 60 more secs.

- Stir in the flour and the beef evenly, and let the contents cook for 60 secs then combine in the cinnamon, bay leaves, stock, and wine.
- Get everything boiling, place a lid on the pot, and put the mix in the oven for 2 hrs.
- Combine in the mint, sun dried tomatoes, and olives.
- Take the dish out of the oven and let everything lose its heat.
- Now set your oven to 400 degrees.
- Coat your 6 pieces of onion with oil and sugar.
- Sear the onions for 60 secs in a skillet then lay out 6 pie dishes.
- Place some beef in each dish and lay your puff pastry over each dish.
- Fold the edges in and place a piece of onion in the middle of each.
- Coat the pies with the eggs and cook them for 30 mins in the oven at 400 degrees.
- Enjoy.

Amount per serving: 6

Timing Information:

Preparation	30 mins
Total Time	32 mins

Nutritional Information:

Calories	2151.4
Cholesterol	202.4mg
Sodium	1504.5mg
Carbohydrates	136.2g
Protein	68.0

* Percent Daily Values are based on a 2,000 calorie diet.

Chipotle Chicken Breast

Ingredients

- 2 tbsps smoked paprika
- 2 cloves garlic, diced
- 1 tsp ground cumin
- 1 tsp caraway seeds
- 1 chipotle pepper in adobo sauce
- 1 tsp harissa
- 4 skinless, boneless chicken breast halves
- 1 tbsp extra-virgin olive oil
- salt and black pepper to taste

Directions

- Get a mortar and pestle and mash the following: adobo sauce, paprika, chipotle pepper, garlic, caraway seeds, and cumin.
- Coat your chicken with this mix, once it is smooth, then place everything in a bowl.
- Place a covering of plastic on the bowl and put everything in the fridge for 5 hrs.
- Get a grill hot and coat the grate with oil, grill your chicken for 6 mins each side, after coating the meat with olive oil, some pepper and salt.

- Enjoy.

Amount per serving (4 total)

Timing Information:

Preparation	20 m
Cooking	10 m
Total Time	4 h 30 m

Nutritional Information:

Calories	178 kcal
Fat	5.6
Carbohydrates	3.2
Protein	28
Cholesterol	68 m
Sodium	101 m

* Percent Daily Values are based on a 2,000 calorie diet.

Paprika Harissa Lemon Fish

Ingredients

- 1 tsp vegetable oil
- 1 lb salmon fillet
- salt and pepper to taste
- 4 thin slices lemon
- 2 thin slices sweet onion, separated into rings
- 1/3 C. mayonnaise
- 1 tsp lemon juice
- 1 tsp harissa
- 1/4 tsp smoked paprika
- 1 tbsp orange juice
- 1 tbsp white wine

Directions

- Grease a casserole dish with oil then set your oven to 425 degrees before doing anything else.
- Coat your salmon with pepper and salt then lay the pieces of fish into the dish. Top the fish with the onion and lemon.
- Get a bowl, combine: paprika, mayo, harissa, and lemon juice.
- Combine the mix until it is smooth then coat your fish with it.

- Add the wine and orange around the fish and cook everything in the oven for 14 mins.
- Now place the fish in a broiler pan and broil everything for 4 mins.
- Enjoy.

Amount per serving (4 total)

Timing Information:

Preparation	20 m
Cooking	15 m
Total Time	35 m

Nutritional Information:

Calories	315 kcal
Fat	22.9 g
Carbohydrates	3.2 mg
Protein	22.9 g
Cholesterol	70 mg
Sodium	262 mg

* Percent Daily Values are based on a 2,000 calorie diet.

Persian Couscous with Harissa and Currants

Ingredients

- 2 tbsps warm water
- 5 saffron threads, or more to taste
- 1 C. couscous
- 1 C. vegetable broth
- 1 celery stalk, diced
- 1/4 C. dried currants
- 2 tbsps extra-virgin olive oil
- 1 tbsp lemon juice
- 1 tsp harissa, or to taste
- 1/2 tsp ground cumin
- sea salt to taste

Directions

- Let your saffron sit submerged in the warm water.
- Get your couscous boiling in the veggie broth.
- Once the mix is boiling place a lid on the pot, shut the heat, and let everything stand for 10 mins.
- Get a bowl, combine: couscous, saffron mix, sea salt, celery, cumin, currants, harissa, olive oil, and lemon juice.
- Place the mix in the fridge for 1 hr.
- Enjoy.

Amount per serving (4 total)

Timing Information:

Preparation	
Cooking	15 m
Total Time	50 m

Nutritional Information:

Calories	265 kcal
Fat	7.3 g
Carbohydrates	43.2 mg
Protein	6.3 g
Cholesterol	0 mg
Sodium	228 mg

* Percent Daily Values are based on a 2,000 calorie diet.

Kale and Sweet Potato Stew

Ingredients

- 1 large onion, diced
- 2 tbsps olive oil
- 8 oz. Spanish chorizo, cut into 1/2 inch pieces
- 3 stalks celery, diced
- 3 carrots, diced
- 2 tsps ground cumin
- 1 tbsp paprika
- 1/2 tsp ground turmeric
- 2 tsps kosher salt
- 1 tsp freshly ground black pepper
- 1 pinch saffron threads
- 5 garlic cloves, diced
- 2 sweet potatoes, peeled and cut into 1-inch pieces
- 8 C. chicken broth
- 4 C. lacinato kale, washed, stemmed, and torn into pieces
- 1 lemon, juiced
- salt and pepper to taste
- 1 pinch harissa, or to taste
- 1 tbsp chopped fresh flat-leaf parsley

Directions

- Stir fry your onions in olive oil, in a large pot, for 10 mins then combine in the chorizo and fry the sausage for 5 more mins.
- Stir in the carrots and celery.
- Continue frying the veggies for 5 mins then combine in: the garlic, cumin, saffron, turmeric, kosher salt, paprika, and black pepper.

- Combine in the spices then continue frying everything for 4 more mins then combine in the broth and sweet potatoes.
- Stir the mix again and get everything boiling.
- Once the mix is boiling, set the heat to low, and simmer the mix for 25 mins.
- Combine in the kale and cook the stew for 12 more mins then add some more pepper, salt, and the lemon juice.
- When serving the stew top it with some parsley and harissa.
- Enjoy.

Amount per serving (8 total)

Timing Information:

Preparation	40 m
Cooking	45 m
Total Time	1 h 25 m

Nutritional Information:

Calories	249 kcal
Fat	15.4 mg
Carbohydrates	18.8 g
Protein	10.4 g
Cholesterol	30 mg
Sodium	1866 mg

* Percent Daily Values are based on a 2,000 calorie diet.

Spicy Carrot Paste

Ingredients

- 4 large carrots, peeled and roughly chopped
- 2 garlic cloves, peeled and chopped
- 1/3 C. olive oil
- 1 tsp harissa
- sea salt
- fresh ground pepper

Directions

- Get your carrots boiling in water.
- Once the carrots are soft remove all the liquids and place them into the bowl of a food processor and add in the garlic.
- Begin to the puree the carrots and garlic then add the oil in a slow stream and continue pureeing the mix.
- Now combine in the harissa and continue to puree everything until you have a smooth paste then add in some pepper and salt.
- Stir the mix for a few secs and serve.
- Enjoy.

Amount per serving: 1

Timing Information:

Preparation	5 mins
Total Time	15 mins

Nutritional Information:

Calories	381.4
Cholesterol	0.0mg
Sodium	100.5mg
Carbohydrates	14.7g
Protein	1.5

* Percent Daily Values are based on a 2,000 calorie diet.

North African Pizza

Ingredients

- 1 pre-baked pizza crust
- 2 tsps berbere
- 1 tsp garlic, diced
- 1/4 tsp salt
- 2 tbsps olive oil
- 1 medium Chinese eggplant, sliced thick
- 1 small zucchini, sliced thick
- 1 small red onion, sliced thick
- 2 tbsps olive oil
- 1 tbsp harissa
- 1 chorizo sausage, sliced
- 6 oz. mozzarella cheese, sliced

Directions

- Set your oven to 350 degrees before doing anything else.
- Combine your olive oil with the salt, garlic, and berbere.
- Stir the mix until it is smooth and the salt has dissolved.
- Now coat your crust with the mix.

- Add your veggies to a casserole dish and top them with some olive oil and the harissa.
- Stir everything again to evenly coat the veggies and cook them in the oven for 22 mins, or until the veggies are tender.
- Let everything lose its heat then place the veggies, cheese, and sausage on the crust.
- Top the crust evenly with the ingredients and cook the pizza for 13 mins in the oven.
- Enjoy.

Amount per serving: 2

Timing Information:

Preparation	15 mins
Total Time	45 mins

Nutritional Information:

Calories	656.9
Cholesterol	93.7mg
Sodium	1202.2mg
Carbohydrates	7.9g
Protein	27.3

* Percent Daily Values are based on a 2,000 calorie diet.

Harissa Burgers

Ingredients

- 1 lb beef sausage meat
- 1 tbsp harissa
- 1 small red onion, chopped
- 1 clove garlic, crushed
- 2 tbsps flat leaf parsley, chopped
- 1 tbsp chopped chives
- 2 tbsps olive oil
- lemon slice, to serve

Directions

- Get a bowl, combine: chives, parsley, garlic, onion, harissa, and sausage.
- Work the mix with your hands then form everything into 8 balls.
- Flatten each ball into a patty and fry each patty for 6 mins per side in hot oil.
- Enjoy.

Amount per serving: 4

Timing Information:

| Preparation | 15 mins |
| Total Time | 35 mins |

Nutritional Information:

Calories	413.4
Cholesterol	81.6mg
Sodium	723.2mg
Carbohydrates	2.0g
Protein	17.4

* Percent Daily Values are based on a 2,000 calorie diet.

Moroccan Style Couscous

Ingredients

- 14 oz. couscous
- 6 scallions, finely sliced
- 3 tbsps mint, roughly chopped
- 9 oz. cherry tomatoes, halved
- 1 3/4 C. vegetable stock, hot
- 1 tsp harissa
- 3 tbsps olive oil
- 1 lemon, juice

Directions

- Get a bowl, combine: tomatoes, couscous, mint, and scallions.
- Stir the mix to evenly distribute the ingredients.
- Now get your veggie stock boiling then combine in the harissa and stir the mix.
- Once the mix is boiling again pour it over your couscous in the bowl.
- Place a covering on the bowl and let the couscous sit for 10 mins.
- Top the mix with some lemon juice and olive oil.
- Enjoy.

Amount per serving: 10

Timing Information:

Preparation	5 mins
Total Time	10 mins

Nutritional Information:

Calories	195.4
Cholesterol	0.0mg
Sodium	7.6mg
Carbohydrates	33.7g
Protein	5.6

* Percent Daily Values are based on a 2,000 calorie diet.

Orange Cinnamon Chicken

Ingredients

- 1/4 C. harissa
- 1/2 C. orange juice
- 1 tbsp grated orange peel
- 1/4 C. cider vinegar
- 2 tbsps vegetable oil
- 2 tsps sugar
- 1 tsp ground cinnamon
- 3 lbs chicken

Directions

- Get a bowl, combine: harissa, orange juice, orange peel, vinegar, veggie oil, sugar, and cinnamon. Stir the mix until it is smooth and even.
- Coat your chicken, between the skin and meat, with some of the mix then place the pieces in a casserole dish.
- Top the chicken with the rest of the mix evenly then place a covering of plastic on the dish.
- Place everything into the fridge for 5 hrs.
- Now set your oven to 350 degrees before doing anything else.
- Remove the covering and cook the chicken in the oven for 2 hrs. Try to baste the chicken every 15 to 20 mins.
- Enjoy.

Amount per serving: 4

Timing Information:

| Preparation | 20 mins |
| Total Time | 2 hrs 20 mins |

Nutritional Information:

Calories	533.3
Cholesterol	155.2mg
Sodium	146.1mg
Carbohydrates	6.2g
Protein	38.7

* Percent Daily Values are based on a 2,000 calorie diet.

Harissa Shrimp and Coriander

Ingredients

- 1/2 C. couscous
- olive oil, for frying
- 1 C. chicken stock
- 1 small onion, sliced
- 2 garlic cloves, crushed
- 1 tsp ground cumin
- 2 C. chopped tomatoes
- 1 tsp harissa
- 1/3 lb raw peeled prawns
- 1 small bunch coriander leaves

Directions

- Get a bowl, combine: 1 tsp olive oil and couscous.
- Get your stock boiling and once it is pour it over your couscous.
- Place a covering of foil on the bowl and let the mix sit for 10 mins.
- At the same time begin to stir fry your garlic and onions in 1 tbsps of oil for 3 mins then combine in the cumin, harissa, and tomatoes, and continue to fry the mix for 60 more secs.
- Add the prawns and cook them until they are fully done for 5 mins then top everything with the coriander.
- Divide your couscous into servings and garnish each one equally with the prawn mix.
- Enjoy.

Amount per serving: 2

Timing Information:

Preparation	5 mins
Total Time	20 mins

Nutritional Information:

Calories	336.1
Cholesterol	97.5mg
Sodium	588.2mg
Carbohydrates	55.4g
Protein	21.6

* Percent Daily Values are based on a 2,000 calorie diet.

Beet Salad

(Tunisian)

Ingredients

- 2 1/2 lbs small red beets, chopped
- 2 tbsps olive oil

Dressing

- 1/2 C. green onion, diced
- 1/4 C. flat-leaf Italian parsley
- 1 garlic clove, diced
- 1 tsp harissa, to taste
- 2 tsps red wine vinegar
- salt & freshly ground black pepper

Directions

- Set your oven to 400 degrees before doing anything else.
- Get a bowl, combine: onions, parsley, garlic clove, harissa, vinegar, some pepper, and some salt. Stir the mix until it is smooth.
- Place your beets in a bowl, top them with olive oil, then place them in a casserole dish. Place a covering of foil around the dish.
- Cook the beets in the oven for 35 mins.
- Once the beets have cooled, combine them with the wet vinegar mix and toss everything.
- Enjoy warm or cold.

Amount per serving: 4

Timing Information:

Preparation	20 mins
Total Time	50 mins

Nutritional Information:

Calories	190.6
Cholesterol	0.0mg
Sodium	229.6mg
Carbohydrates	29.0g
Protein	5.1

* Percent Daily Values are based on a 2,000 calorie diet.

Spicy Cauliflower

Ingredients

- 1 head cauliflower, florets separated, stems chopped
- 2 tbsps olive oil
- 1/2 tsp salt
- 1 tsp cumin seed
- chopped cilantro or flat leaf parsley

Spicy Mayo:

- 1 C. mayonnaise
- 1 tsp harissa

Directions

- Get a bowl, combine: mayo and harissa. Stir the mix until it is smooth. Place a covering of plastic on the bowl and put everything in the fridge for 60 mins.
- Set your oven to 425 degrees before doing anything else.
- Lay your florets in a casserole dish and top them with olive oil.
- Now top the veggies with the cumin seeds and salt.
- Cook everything in the oven for 12 mins then stir the florets and continue baking them for 17 more mins.
- Place the florets in a bowl and cover them with the cilantro and the harissa mix.
- Enjoy.

Amount per serving: 4

Timing Information:

Preparation	15 mins
Total Time	45 mins

Nutritional Information:

Calories	327.5
Cholesterol	15.2mg
Sodium	753.5mg
Carbohydrates	21.5g
Protein	3.4

* Percent Daily Values are based on a 2,000 calorie diet.

Mushroom Kebabs

Ingredients

- 1/2 tbsp harissa
- 1 tbsp olive oil
- 2 tbsps balsamic vinegar
- 1 tsp dried oregano
- 8 oz. baby portabella mushrooms, halved lengthwise

Directions

- Get a bowl, combine: oregano, harissa, balsamic, and olive oil.
- Combine the mix until it is smooth then combine in the mushrooms and stir the mix again to evenly coat the mushrooms.
- Place a covering of plastic on the bowl and let it stand for 40 mins.
- Now set your oven to 350 degrees before doing anything else.
- Place your mushrooms onto skewers that have been soaked in water for 20 mins then cook the mushrooms in the oven for 15 mins.
- Enjoy.

Amount per serving: 4

Timing Information:

Preparation	10 mins
Total Time	20 mins

Nutritional Information:

Calories	50.0
Cholesterol	0.0mg
Sodium	7.0mg
Carbohydrates	3.7g
Protein	1.2

* Percent Daily Values are based on a 2,000 calorie diet.

Classical Moroccan Tagine I

Ingredients

- 2 tbsps olive oil
- 1/2 onion, chopped
- 1 (15 oz.) cans chickpeas, drained & rinsed
- 1 (15 oz.) cans diced tomatoes
- 1 tbsp fresh Italian parsley, finely chopped
- 1 tbsp fresh cilantro, finely chopped
- 1/4 tsp salt
- 1/4 tsp black pepper
- 1/4 tsp harissa
- 1/4 tsp cinnamon
- 1/4 tsp turmeric
- 1/4 tsp ginger
- 1/4 tsp cumin

Directions

- Place your onions in bowl and top them with the oil. Then add in: the chickpeas, diced tomatoes, parsley, cilantro, salt, black pepper, harissa, cinnamon, turmeric, ginger, and cumin.
- Stir the mix until the onions are evenly coated then place everything into a tagine.
- Place a covering on the tagine and cook the mix for 35 mins with a low level of heat.
- Enjoy.

Amount per serving: 2

Timing Information:

Preparation	5 mins
Total Time	35 mins

Nutritional Information:

Calories	426.6
Cholesterol	0.0mg
Sodium	940.4mg
Carbohydrates	59.9g
Protein	12.9

* Percent Daily Values are based on a 2,000 calorie diet.

Vegan Zucchini (Tunisian)

Ingredients

- 1/2 lb zucchini
- 2 carrots
- 2 tbsps olive oil
- 1 garlic clove, diced
- 1/2 tbsp harissa
- 1/4 tsp ground cumin
- 1/4 tsp caraway seed
- juice of half lemon
- plain yogurt
- fresh cilantro
- salt, to taste
- black pepper, to taste

Directions

- Get a bowl, combine: olive oil, garlic clove, harissa, cumin, caraway, and lemon juice.

- Get a casserole dish and place your carrots and zucchini in it. Top them with the olive oil mix evenly then place a covering of plastic on the dish and let the veggie sit for 60 mins.
- Now get a grill hot and coat the grate with oil.
- Grill the veggies for about 10 mins or until you find that the outside is slightly charred but the inside is tender.
- Place the veggies in a dish for serving then top them with some pepper and salt.
- Now add your cilantro evenly over everything and serve the dish with some yogurt.
- Enjoy.

Amount per serving: 3

Timing Information:

Preparation	15 mins
Total Time	25 mins

Nutritional Information:

Calories	111.8
Cholesterol	0.0mg
Sodium	34.8mg
Carbohydrates	6.7g
Protein	1.4

* Percent Daily Values are based on a 2,000 calorie diet.

Beef Koftas
(Moroccan Style)

Ingredients

- 1 bunch of fresh mint, finely chopped
- 1 lb ground beef
- 1 tbsp thyme
- 1 tbsp oregano
- 1 onion, finely chopped
- 1 tsp ground cumin
- 1/4 tsp harissa
- salt

Directions

- Get a bowl, combine: beef, mint, thyme, oregano, onion, cumin, harissa, and some salt.
- Work the mix with your hands then place everything into balls.
- Now get some olive oil hot and begin to fry your meatballs for 12 mins.
- Enjoy.

Amount per serving: 4

Timing Information:

| Preparation | 10 mins |
| Total Time | 20 mins |

Nutritional Information:

Calories	257.7
Cholesterol	77.1mg
Sodium	76.9mg
Carbohydrates	3.0g
Protein	21.5

* Percent Daily Values are based on a 2,000 calorie diet.

Harissa Ginger and Cinnamon Lamb (Moroccan)

Ingredients

- 2 lamb fillets
- 1 tsp ground cumin
- 1 tsp paprika
- 3 garlic cloves, crushed
- 1 tsp ground coriander
- 1 tsp dried parsley flakes
- 1/2 tsp cinnamon
- 1/2 tsp ground ginger
- 1 tsp sugar
- 1/2 tsp harissa
- 2 tbsps lemon juice
- 2 tbsps olive oil

Directions

- Get a bowl, combine: cumin, paprika, garlic cloves, coriander, parsley, cinnamon, ginger, sugar, harissa, lemon juice, and olive oil.
- Stir the mix until it is smooth then evenly coat your lamb with the mix.
- Cook the lamb for 7 mins each side in oil.
- Then the meat with foil and let it stand for 7 mins.
- Now cut your lamb into servings.
- Enjoy.

Amount per serving: 2

Timing Information:

| Preparation | 8 mins |
| Total Time | 18 mins |

Nutritional Information:

Calories	151.1
Cholesterol	0.0mg
Sodium	4.5mg
Carbohydrates	7.3g
Protein	0.8

* Percent Daily Values are based on a 2,000 calorie diet.

Potatoes from Tunisia

Ingredients

- 12 oz. potatoes, Chopped
- 1 medium red onion, Chopped
- 3 tbsps olive oil
- 2 garlic cloves, Finely Chopped
- 4 medium eggs
- 1 tsp harissa
- 1 bunch cilantro
- 1 bunch parsley
- salt and pepper

Directions

- Begin to stir fry your onions in 2 tbsps of olive oil for 7 mins then combine in the garlic and continue cooking everything for 3 more mins.
- Get your potatoes boiling in water until they are soft. Then remove all the liquids and mash the potatoes.
- Now add in the garlic and onions and stir everything together.
- Get a bowl, combine, salt, eggs, parsley, harissa, and cilantro. Work this mix into your potatoes slowly.
- Now get the rest of the oil hot then layer your potato mix into the pan.

- With a low level of heat, cook the bottom, then place the entire pan under the broiler until the top is browned.
- Enjoy.

Amount per serving: 4

Timing Information:

| Preparation | 40 mins |
| Total Time | 55 mins |

Nutritional Information:

Calories	233.7
Cholesterol	163.6mg
Sodium	73.9mg
Carbohydrates	18.6g
Protein	7.8

* Percent Daily Values are based on a 2,000 calorie diet.

Spicy Garbanzo Dip

Ingredients

- 2 C. dried garbanzo beans
- 1 carrot, peeled and cut in half
- 1 medium Spanish onion, cut in half
- 4 garlic cloves, peeled
- 2 eggplants, cut in half lengthwise
- 1/4 C. olive oil
- 2 birds eye chilies, cut in half, seeds removed
- 2 tbsps olive oil
- 1 tsp harissa
- 1 tsp ground cumin

Directions

- Let your chickpeas sit submerged in water overnight. Then remove all the liquids.
- Get the following boiling in water, in a large pot: 4 C. of water, chickpeas, onions, and carrots.
- Once the mix is boiling, set the heat to low, and let the contents cook for 90 mins.
- Set your oven to 300 degrees before doing anything else.

- Now place one C. of the liquid to the side and remove the rest.
- Get a bowl, combine: 1/4 C. of olive oil, eggplant, and garlic.
- Stir the mix to evenly coat everything then place the mix into a casserole dish.
- Cook the eggplants in the oven for 50 mins then add the chilies to the dish and keep cooking the mix for 12 more mins.
- Remove the insides of your eggplant and place them into the bowl of a food processor.
- Combine in the 3 tsp of the reserved liquid, garlic and chilies, 2 tbsp olive oil, cumin, harissa, and chickpeas.
- Process the mix into a smooth paste and add in some more of the reserved liquid if needed. The mix should be creamy.
- Serve the mix with some toasted pita rounds.
- Enjoy.

Amount per serving: 1

Timing Information:

Preparation	8 hrs 9 hrs
Total Time	30 mins

Nutritional Information:

Calories	840.8
Cholesterol	0.0mg
Sodium	58.1mg
Carbohydrates	108.1g
Protein	30.3

* Percent Daily Values are based on a 2,000 calorie diet.

Pistachio and Fig Tagine

Ingredients

- 2 tbsps olive oil
- 2 tsps ground coriander
- 2 tsps ground cumin
- 1 1/2 tsps ground cinnamon
- 1 1/2 tsps turmeric
- 1 tsp grated lemon, zest of
- 1 1/2 tbsps lemon juice
- 1 1/2 tsps harissa
- 8 chicken thighs, skin removed
- 2 tbsps olive oil
- 2 onions, chopped
- 2 carrots, sliced into coins
- 2 cloves garlic, diced
- 2 tsps grated ginger
- 6 oz. button mushrooms, halved
- 8 large dried figs, coarsely chopped
- 2 tbsps all-purpose flour
- 1 3/4 C. chicken stock
- 2 tbsps tomato paste
- 1 tbsp lemon juice
- 3/4 C. pitted black olives
- 1/3 C. shelled pistachios
- 2 tbsps chopped fresh parsley

Directions

- Get a bowl, combine: harissa, 2 tbsps olive oil, lemon juice, coriander, lemon zest, cumin, turmeric, and cinnamon.
- Stir the mix until it is smooth then cover your pieces of chicken with it.
- Sear the chicken all over then place the meat in the crock of a slow cooker.

- Begin to fry your garlic, carrots, and onions for 7 mins then add in the flour, figs, and mushrooms.
- Stir the mix and continue to cook everything for 2 more mins.
- Now combine in the lemon juice, tomato paste, and chicken stock.
- Stir the mix again and get everything boiling.
- Once the mix is boiling pour everything in the slow cooker.
- Place a lid on the crock pot and cook everything for 4 hrs with a high level of heat.
- When 30 mins of cooking time is left, add in your pistachios, parsley, and olives to the slow cooker and let everything finish simmering.
- Enjoy.

Amount per serving: 4

Timing Information:

Preparation	25 mins
Total Time	3 hrs 40 mins

Nutritional Information:

Calories	767.0
Cholesterol	161.0mg
Sodium	573.4mg
Carbohydrates	37.0g
Protein	41.6g

* Percent Daily Values are based on a 2,000 calorie diet.

Countryside Beef

(Tunisia)

Ingredients

- 1 lb stew meat, cut into 1-inch cubes
- 2 tbsps tabil, (crushed coriander seeds, cumin, caraway, red pepper)
- 1/2 tsp black pepper
- 1/4 C. extra virgin olive oil, plus
- 2 tbsps extra virgin olive oil
- 1 onion, chopped
- 1 lb fresh tomato, chopped
- 1 1/2 C. water
- 2 tsps harissa, Harissa Paste
- 1/2 C. canned chick-peas
- 2 tsps cayenne pepper
- 1 1/2 lbs turnips, peeled and quartered
- 2/3 C. parsley, finely chopped
- 10 oz. spinach, cut into strips
- 2 tsps kosher salt
- 1 lemon, juice of

Directions

- Get a bowl, combine: black pepper and tabil.
- Place the beef into the spice and evenly coat everything.
- Place the meat into a large pan and sear it all over with the onions for 7 mins then combine in the cayenne, tomatoes, chickpeas, 1 C. of water, and harissa.

- Get everything boiling, place a lid on the pot, set the heat to low, and let everything cook for 90 mins.
- Now combine in more black pepper, the rest of the water, salt, turnips, spinach, and parsley.
- Let the mix continue to cook for 60 more mins then add in the lemon juice.
- Enjoy.

Amount per serving: 4

Timing Information:

Preparation	30 mins
Total Time	2 hrs 30 mins

Nutritional Information:

Calories	605.3
Cholesterol	75.9mg
Sodium	1210.2mg
Carbohydrates	29.8g
Protein	27.4

* Percent Daily Values are based on a 2,000 calorie diet.

Harissa Pasta

Ingredients

- 1 onion
- 1 crushed garlic clove
- 1 tbsp tomato paste
- 28 oz. chopped tomatoes
- salt and pepper
- 1/2 tsp harissa
- 2 tbsps fresh basil, chopped
- 2 tbsps fresh parsley, chopped
- 1/2 tsp sugar
- 2 C. chopped cooked chicken
- 2 C. uncooked pasta
- 1 C. cottage cheese
- 1 egg
- 1/2 C. grated parmesan cheese
- 1 1/2 C. shredded cheese
- Non-stick spray

Directions

- Begin to stir fry your onions in some oil for 5 mins then combine in the tomato puree and continue frying the mix for 3 more mins.
- Now combine in the sugar, harissa, chopped tomatoes, some pepper, and the parsley / basil.
- Place a lid on the pot and gently boil the mix for 20 mins.
- At the same time get your pasta boiling in water and salt for 9 mins then remove all the liquids.
- Get a bowl, combine: parmesan, cottage cheese, and eggs.
- Set your oven to 350 degrees before doing anything else.

- Now get a baking dish, grease it, then combine in your tomato sauce, chicken and pasta in a bowl.
- Add half of this mix to the baking dish then top the contents with the cheese mix.
- Now layer half a C. of shredded cheese over everything then add the rest of the chicken pasta mix.
- Top the entire dish with another C. of shredded cheese and cook everything in the oven for 50 mins.
- Enjoy.

Amount per serving: 4

Timing Information:

| Preparation | 30 mins |
| Total Time | 1 hr 15 mins |

Nutritional Information:

Calories	607.0
Cholesterol	146.0mg
Sodium	908.5mg
Carbohydrates	52.6g
Protein	46.4

* Percent Daily Values are based on a 2,000 calorie diet.

Harissa Dump Dinner

Ingredients

- 2 lbs pork tenderloin
- 1/4 C. low soy sauce
- 1 tbsp yellow mustard
- 2 tbsps maple syrup
- 1 tbsp olive oil
- 2 chopped shallots
- 1/2 C. chicken broth
- 2 garlic cloves, crushed
- 1/4 tsp harissa
- 1 C. chopped mushroom
- 20 small potatoes
- 1/4 tsp salt
- 1/2 tsp pepper

Directions

- Brown your pork all over in hot oil then put it in the crock pot.
- Get a bowl, combine: pepper, syrup, salt, soya sauce, chicken broth, mustard, and harissa.
- Begin to stir fry your mushrooms, garlic, and shallots for 5 mins then add in the harissa mix and stir everything.
- Add this mix into the crock pot again and stir everything one more time.
- Place the lid on the slow cooker and let the mix cook for 7 hrs with a low level of heat.
- When 60 mins of cooking time is left combine in the potatoes.
- Enjoy.

Amount per serving: 4

Timing Information:

Preparation	10 m
Total Time	2 h

Nutritional Information:

Calories	1012.5
Cholesterol	147.5mg
Sodium	985.1mg
Carbohydrates	159.8g
Protein	66.5

* Percent Daily Values are based on a 2,000 calorie diet.

Mediterranean Mango Salad

Ingredients

- 1 (15 oz.) cans black beans, rinsed well and drained
- 1 avocado, peeled and diced into 1 inch pieces
- 1 mango, peeled and diced into 1 inch pieces
- 4 green onions, chopped
- 1 red bell pepper, chopped
- 1/2 C. frozen corn
- 1/4 C. chopped parsley
- 2 tbsps fresh-squeezed lemon juice
- 1 tbsp white balsamic vinegar
- 1/4 tsp harissa
- salt, to taste to taste
- 2 tbsps good-quality olive oil

Directions

- Get a bowl, combine: pepper, lemon juice, salt, olive oil, balsamic, and harissa.
- Get a 2nd bowl, combine: onions, avocado, pepper, black beans, mango, and corn.
- Top the mix with the olive oil mix and place a covering of plastic on the bowl.
- Put everything in the fridge until it is chilled.
- Enjoy.

Amount per serving: 6

Timing Information:

| Preparation | 30 mins |
| Total Time | 30 mins |

Nutritional Information:

Calories	256.2
Cholesterol	0.0mg
Sodium	9.5mg
Carbohydrates	37.6g
Protein	7.5

* Percent Daily Values are based on a 2,000 calorie diet.

Lentils and Shrimp

Ingredients

- 1 tbsp olive oil
- 1 small onion, finely chopped
- 1 chorizo sausage, chopped
- 1 tbsp harissa
- 1 can tomatoes, chopped
- 2 cans brown lentils, rinsed, drained
- 1 jar roasted red peppers, drained, sliced
- 1 C. chicken stock
- 1 lb peeled prawns, tails intact
- 1/4 C. chopped flat-leaf Italian parsley
- to serve
- crusty bread
- mixed salad leaves

Directions

- Stir fry your onions and chorizo in 1 tbsp of oil for 7 mins then combine in the harissa and continue frying everything for 60 more secs.
- Add in the red peppers, lentils, and tomatoes.

- Get everything boiling, set the heat to low, and let the mix gently cook for 25 mins.
- Top your fish with some black pepper and sea salt then add them to the simmering mix.
- Place a lid on the pan and let the contents cook for 7 mins.
- Combine in the parsley and divide the mix between serving dishes.
- Place some bread into each dish.
- Enjoy.

Amount per serving: 4

Timing Information:

| Preparation | 20 mins |
| Total Time | 50 mins |

Nutritional Information:

Calories	1001.4
Cholesterol	205.0mg
Sodium	480.7mg
Carbohydrates	133.3g
Protein	84.0

* Percent Daily Values are based on a 2,000 calorie diet.

Creamy Chicken Quarters

Ingredients

- 3 1/4 lbs chicken, quartered
- 1 tbsp corn flour
- 1 C. plain yogurt
- 1 tbsp harissa
- 1/3 C. mint, shredded
- 2 tsps ground cumin
- salt and pepper

Directions

- Set your oven to 400 degrees before doing anything else.
- Add the following to the bowl of a food processor: salt, corn flour, pepper, yogurt, cumin, harissa, and mint.
- Process the mix until it is smooth.
- Now coat your chicken with the harissa mix evenly then place everything on a rack.
- Place the rack in a roasting pan and put everything the oven for 30 mins.
- Enjoy.

Amount per serving: 4

Timing Information:

| Preparation | 8 mins |
| Total Time | 43 mins |

Nutritional Information:

Calories	843.6
Cholesterol	284.3mg
Sodium	290.2mg
Carbohydrates	5.3g
Protein	71.2

* Percent Daily Values are based on a 2,000 calorie diet.

Orange and Pine Nut Fish

Ingredients

- 1/2 lb filleted mackerel
- 2 tbsps plain flour
- 1/2 tsp smoked paprika
- 2 tbsps extra virgin olive oil
- 1 small orange, juice and zest
- 1 tsp harissa
- 1/4 C. pine nuts, toasted
- 1 bunch coriander, chopped

Directions

- Combine your paprika and flour then coat your fish with the mix and place everything in a casserole dish.
- Get a bowl, combine: harissa, 1 tbsp olive oil, orange juice, and orange zest.
- Stir the mix until it is smooth.
- Now begin to fry your fish in the rest of the olive oil for 6 mins each side, then top the fish with the orange mix and get everything boiling.
- Let the mix simmer for a few mins then top everything with the coriander and pine nuts.
- Enjoy.

Amount per serving: 2

Timing Information:

Preparation	5 mins
Total Time	15 mins

Nutritional Information:

Calories	674.0
Cholesterol	105.0mg
Sodium	137.6mg
Carbohydrates	21.6g
Protein	33.2

* Percent Daily Values are based on a 2,000 calorie diet.

Shakshouka

(Spicy Poached Eggs in Tomato Sauce)

(Algerian)

Ingredients

- 3 tbsps olive oil
- 1/2 tsp cumin seed
- 1 tbsp paprika
- 1 onion, thinly sliced
- 1 tbsp harissa
- 2 garlic cloves, diced
- 3 tomatoes, peeled, seeded and diced
- 1 potato, small diced cubes
- 1 green bell pepper, diced
- 1 red bell pepper, diced
- 1 yellow bell pepper, diced
- 1 chili pepper
- 1 C. water
- kosher salt
- fresh ground pepper
- 4 eggs
- parsley or cilantro, chopped
- black olives
- capers

Directions

- Toast your cumin for 30 secs, in oil, then add in the paprika and cook everything for 20 more secs.

- Combine in the harissa, garlic, and onions and continue frying everything for 7 mins then add the tomatoes and get everything boiling.
- Once the mix is boiling, combine in the pepper, water, diced chili peppers, and potatoes.
- Get everything boiling again.
- Once the mix is boiling again, set the heat to low, place a lid on the pot, and continue to cook everything for 12 mins.
- Now cut an opening into your peppers.
- Get a little bowl and add one egg to it.
- Place the egg into the peppers one after the other and place the lid back on the pot. Continue cooking everything for 12 more mins.
- Top everything with the cilantro, capers, and olives.
- Enjoy.

Amount per serving: 4

Timing Information:

| Preparation | 10 mins |
| Total Time | 30 mins |

Nutritional Information:

Calories	252.8
Cholesterol	186.0mg
Sodium	85.8mg
Carbohydrates	20.5g
Protein	9.4

* Percent Daily Values are based on a 2,000 calorie diet.

North African Breakfast

Ingredients

- 1 lb carrot, sliced
- 1 tbsp caraway seed, freshly ground
- 1 tbsp harissa
- 4 large garlic cloves, diced
- 1/2 tsp salt
- pepper, freshly ground
- 8 large eggs, fresh
- 2 eggs, hard cooked and finely chopped
- 1/4 C. fresh flat-leaf parsley, chopped
- 1 tbsp extra virgin olive oil

Directions

- Get your oven's broiler hot and begin to steam your carrots over 2 inches of boiling water, with a steamer insert, for 25 mins, with a lid on the pot.
- Add the carrots to the bowl of a food processor and begin to puree them, combine in some pepper, some salt, caraway, garlic, and the harissa.
- Continue to puree the mix until it is smooth.
- Get a bowl, combine: 1/2 tsp salt and the eggs.
- Whisk the eggs evenly then add in the carrot mix and hard boiled eggs.

- Stir the mix again then add in the parsley.
- Get your olive oil hot then begin to fry the egg mix for 5 mins then place everything under the broiler for 5 more mins.
- Enjoy.

Amount per serving: 6

Timing Information:

Preparation	15 mins
Total Time	45 mins

Nutritional Information:

Calories	178.2
Cholesterol	310.0mg
Sodium	366.3mg
Carbohydrates	9.3g
Protein	11.6

* Percent Daily Values are based on a 2,000 calorie diet.

Mediterranean Vegetarian Tagine

Ingredients

- 2 tbsps olive oil
- 1 tsp cardamom seed
- 1 cinnamon stick
- 1 large onion, diced
- 1 large eggplant, diced
- 2 garlic cloves, crushed
- 2 tbsps harissa
- 1 can diced tomatoes
- 1/2 C. vegetable stock
- 2 tbsps honey, plus
- extra honey, to drizzle
- 2 tbsps of fresh mint, diced

Directions

- Fry your cinnamon and cardamom in oil for 1 min then add in the eggplants and onions.
- Continue to fry everything for 5 more mins then combine in the stock, garlic, tomatoes, and harissa.
- Let everything simmer for 12 mins then add some pepper, salt, and honey. Stir the honey and spices then shut the heat.
- When serving the tagine top each plate with more honey and some mint.
- Enjoy.

Amount per serving: 4

Timing Information:

| Preparation | 10 mins |
| Total Time | 25 mins |

Nutritional Information:

Calories	187.3
Cholesterol	0.0mg
Sodium	12.0mg
Carbohydrates	30.5g
Protein	3.7

* Percent Daily Values are based on a 2,000 calorie diet.

Classical Lentils

Ingredients

- 2 large onions, diced
- 2 large carrots, peeled and diced
- 2 celery ribs, diced
- 1 tbsp oil
- 3 garlic cloves, finely chopped
- 1 1/2 C. green lentils
- 3 small red chilies
- 1 tsp harissa
- 1 tsp ground cumin
- 2 can chopped tomatoes with juice
- 2 C. vegetable stock
- 2 cans red kidney beans, rinsed and drained
- 2 tbsps concentrated tomato paste
- salt
- ground black pepper

Directions

- Begin to stir fry your carrots, onions, and celery, in oil for 10 mins then combine in the chili, garlic, harissa, and cumin.
- Let the mix continue to cook for 60 secs then combine in the stock, lentils, tomato paste, and chopped tomatoes.
- Get the mix boiling, set the heat to low, and let everything gently cook for 10 mins.
- Now place the mix into the crock pot of a slow cooker and place a lid on the crock pot.
- Let the content cook for 7 hrs with low level of heat.

- When 1 hour is left of cooking time add in your kidney beans some pepper and salt.
- Enjoy.

Amount per serving: 6

Timing Information:

Preparation	15 mins
Total Time	6 hrs 15 mins

Nutritional Information:

Calories	438.7
Cholesterol	0.0mg
Sodium	326.5mg
Carbohydrates	78.0g
Protein	26.3

* Percent Daily Values are based on a 2,000 calorie diet.

Balsamic Bake

Ingredients

- 3/4 tsp crushed red pepper flakes
- 1 tsp cumin seed
- 1 tsp coriander seed
- 1 tsp fennel seed
- 1/4 tsp ground cinnamon
- 1/4 C. honey
- 1/2 C. balsamic vinegar
- 3/4 C. virgin olive oil
- 1 small eggplant, cut into 1 1/2 pieces
- 1 small yellow pepper, cut into chunks
- 1 small red pepper, cut into chunks
- 1 small onion, cut into chunks
- 2 small zucchini, cut into chunks
- 1 (15 oz.) cans chickpeas, rinsed and drained
- 1/2 C. sliced almonds, toasted
- fresh cilantro
- harissa

Directions

- Set your oven to 450 degrees before doing anything else.
- Add the following to the bowl of a food processor: fennel, pepper flakes coriander, and cumin.
- Process the mix a few times then combine in the vinegar, cinnamon, honey, salt, and pepper.

- Continue to pulse the mix then add in the oil gradually and let the processor run on a low speed.
- Get a bowl, combine: zucchini, eggplant, onion, and peppers.
- Stir the mix then place the veggies in a casserole dish cook them in the oven for 22 mins.
- Stir the veggies every 6 mins.
- Now get a 2nd bowl and place your chickpeas in them.
- Once the veggies are done cooking add them to the bowl with the chickpeas then add in the cilantro and almonds.
- Stir the mix gently then combine in the harissa and stir everything again.
- Enjoy.

Amount per serving: 4

Timing Information:

Preparation	20 mins
Total Time	40 mins

Nutritional Information:

Calories	717.2
Cholesterol	0.0mg
Sodium	338.4mg
Carbohydrates	65.7g
Protein	11.1

* Percent Daily Values are based on a 2,000 calorie diet.

Moroccan Parsnips

Ingredients

- 2 lbs small parsnips, sliced
- 3 tbsps olive oil
- 1 small onion, finely chopped
- 1 garlic clove, finely chopped
- 1 tbsp harissa
- 1 tsp cumin
- 1 tsp ground coriander
- 1 tsp honey
- 2/3 C. vegetable broth
- salt and pepper
- cilantro

Directions

- Get your parsnips boiling in water for 8 mins then remove all the liquids.
- Begin to stir fry your garlic and onions in oil for 7 mins then add in the seasonings, harissa, parsnips, honey, and broth.
- Get everything boiling, set the heat to medium / low and let the contents cook for 12 mins.
- Enjoy.

Amount per serving: 4

Timing Information:

Preparation	5 mins
Total Time	20 mins

Nutritional Information:

Calories	276.7
Cholesterol	0.0mg
Sodium	24.8mg
Carbohydrates	44.7g
Protein	3.1

* Percent Daily Values are based on a 2,000 calorie diet.

Coconut Ceviche

(Morocco)

Ingredients

- 2 tsps harissa
- 1/2 C. unsweetened coconut milk
- 1/2 C. fresh lemon juice
- 1/4 C. fresh lime juice
- 1/4 C. fresh orange juice
- 2 lbs sea bass, diced
- 1/4 C. red onion, finely chopped
- 1 tsp diced fresh ginger root
- 2 tbsps extra-virgin olive oil
- 2 tbsps chopped Moroccan preserved lemon
- 1 tbsp caraway seed, lightly toasted and then crushed
- 1/2 tsp ground cumin
- 2 tbsps chopped fresh chervil
- kosher salt to taste

Directions

- Get a bowl, combine: orange juice, harissa, lime juice, coconut milk, and lemon juice.
- Stir the mix until it is smooth then combine in the chervil, fish, cumin, onion, caraway, ginger, lemon, and olive oil.
- Stir the mix again the place a covering of plastic on the bowl.
- Put everything the fridge for 4 hours until the fish is white then add some additional harissa and salt.

- Enjoy.

Amount per serving (6 total)

Timing Information:

Preparation	20 m
Cooking	3 h
Total Time	3 h 20 m

Nutritional Information:

Calories	250 kcal
Fat	11.8 m
Carbohydrates	7g
Protein	28.8 g
Cholesterol	62 mg
Sodium	458 mg

* Percent Daily Values are based on a 2,000 calorie diet.

North African Style Dip

Ingredients

- 2 lbs bulk spicy pork sausage
- 1 onion, diced
- 3 tbsps butter
- 2 tbsps all-purpose flour
- 3 cloves garlic, diced
- 8 fluid oz. half-and-half
- 2 (8 oz.) packages cream cheese, cut into chunks
- 12 oz. ajvar sauce
- 1 tsp harissa

Directions

- Begin to stir fry your onions and sausage for 12 mins then remove the meat and onions from the pan.
- Add the butter to the same pan and let it melt.
- Once the butter has melted combine in the flour and garlic.
- Stir the mix and heat everything for 7 mins.
- Now combine in the half and half and stir everything then add the ajvar and cream cheese.
- Stir and heat the mix for 6 mins then combine in the sausage mix and harissa.
- Stir everything and get the mix hot.
- Enjoy.

Amount per serving (12 total)

Timing Information:

Preparation	5 m
Cooking	20 m
Total Time	25 m

Nutritional Information:

Calories	393 kcal
Fat	33.5 mg
Carbohydrates	9.7 g
Protein	14.3 g
Cholesterol	97 mg
Sodium	719 mg

* Percent Daily Values are based on a 2,000 calorie diet.

Tomato Shrimp

Ingredients

- 3 tbsps butter
- 1 C. finely chopped onion
- 2 cloves garlic, diced
- 3 large ripe tomatoes, peeled, seeded, and chopped
- 1/2 tsp dried oregano
- 1 tbsp harissa
- salt & fresh ground pepper
- 2 lbs large shrimp, peeled and deveined
- 1 tbsp diced fresh parsley

Directions

- Set your oven to 375 degrees before doing anything else.
- Get your onions frying in butter for 8 mins with a lid on the pot.
- Combine in the harissa, garlic, oregano, and tomatoes.
- Let the mix cook for 12 mins then add in some pepper and salt.
- Stir the mix then enter everything into a casserole dish.
- Coat your shrimp with some pepper and salt then add your shrimp to the dish as well.
- Cook everything in the oven for 12 mins then top the dish with the parsley.

- Enjoy.

Amount per serving: 4

Timing Information:

Preparation	30 mins
Total Time	57 mins

Nutritional Information:

Calories	361.7
Cholesterol	368.5mg
Sodium	406.6mg
Carbohydrates	12.1g
Protein	47.9

* Percent Daily Values are based on a 2,000 calorie diet.

Harissa Crab Bake

Ingredients

- 1 1/2 lbs lump crabmeat, picked over
- 8 C. day-old white bread, cubes
- 3 C. warm water
- 3 tbsps butter
- 1 onion, diced small
- 1 red bell pepper, diced small
- 3 medium carrots, peeled and coarsely grated
- 3 garlic cloves, diced
- 1 tsp ground cumin
- 1 tsp dried oregano
- 1 tsp sweet paprika
- salt and pepper
- 2 C. milk
- 1/4 C. heavy cream
- 1/2 C. dry white wine
- 1 1/2 tbsps harissa
- 2/3 C. fresh parmesan cheese, grated

Directions

- Get a bowl, combine: water and the pieces of bread. Leave the mix for 30 mins.
- Squeeze the bread together to remove all the liquids then break it into pieces.
- Set your oven to 375 degrees before doing anything else.
- Now get your butter hot and begin to stir fry your bell pepper and onions for 5 mins in the butter.
- Now combine in the pepper, carrots, salt, cumin, garlic, paprika, and oregano.

- Stir fry everything for 60 more secs then combine in the wine, bread, cream, and milk.
- Continue to fry everything for 7 more mins then combine in the crab, stir the mix, then shut the heat.
- Top everything with the harissa, some pepper and salt as well.
- Then place the mix in a casserole dish.
- Cover everything with the cheese and cook the dish in the oven for 22 mins.
- Enjoy.

Amount per serving: 8

Timing Information:

| Preparation | 40 mins |
| Total Time | 1 hr 15 mins |

Nutritional Information:

Calories	533.6
Cholesterol	102.0mg
Sodium	1051.5mg
Carbohydrates	60.2g
Protein	32.7

* Percent Daily Values are based on a 2,000 calorie diet.

East African Penne

(Ethiopian)

Ingredients

- 1 lb Yukon gold potato, peeled
- 1/4 C. extra virgin olive oil, divided
- 1/2 C. blanched almonds
- 1/4 C. shallot, thinly sliced
- 2 garlic cloves, diced
- 1/4 C. fresh lemon juice
- 2 tbsps fresh parmesan cheese, grated
- 2 tbsps harissa
- 1 tsp salt
- 6 C. hot cooked penne
- 1/4 C. arugula, chopped
- 1/4 C. basil, chopped

Directions

- Get your potatoes boiling in water and salt for 20 mins then remove all the liquids save 1.5 cups of it placed to side.
- Cut your potatoes into bite sized pieces.

- Now begin to stir fry your garlic, shallots, and almonds in 1 tbsp of oil for 10 mins then put everything into the bowl of a food processor and also add in: the salt, 1 tbsp oil, harissa, cheese, and juice.
- Puree the mix then add the 1.5 C. of water and continue to puree everything for 2 more mins.
- Get a bowl, combine: shallot mix, potatoes, and pasta. Stir the pasta mix.
- Now add in the arugula and stir everything again.
- Top the dish with the basil.
- Enjoy.

Amount per serving: 4

Timing Information:

| Preparation | 20 mins |
| Total Time | 1 hr |

Nutritional Information:

Calories	609.3
Cholesterol	2.7mg
Sodium	641.5mg
Carbohydrates	85.8g
Protein	18.8

* Percent Daily Values are based on a 2,000 calorie diet.

Mediterranean Meatballs

Ingredients

- 1/2 lb lb ground pork
- 1/2 lb diced beef
- 1 onion, finely chopped
- 3 garlic cloves, crushed
- 3/4 tsp harissa
- 1 tsp sweet paprika
- 1/2 tsp smoked paprika
- 1/2 tsp cayenne pepper
- 1 tsp thyme
- 1/2 tsp baking powder
- 1 tsp soaked and ground caraway
- 1 tsp marjoram
- salt & freshly ground black pepper, to taste
- 1/2 tsp allspice
- chicken stock
- 1 tbsp olive oil

Directions

- Get a bowl, combine: pork, beef, onion, garlic, harissa, paprika, thyme, baking powder, thyme, cayenne, caraway, marjoram, some salt, some pepper, and some salt. Work the mix with your hands then form everything into small hot dogs.
- Fry the meat with a medium level of heat for 25 mins.
- Enjoy.

Amount per serving: 4

Timing Information:

Preparation	10 mins
Total Time	30 mins

Nutritional Information:

Calories	348.6
Cholesterol	87.5mg
Sodium	124.0mg
Carbohydrates	4.4g
Protein	22.8

* Percent Daily Values are based on a 2,000 calorie diet.

Pumpkin Tagine

Ingredients

- 2 tbsps olive oil
- 1 large onion, roughly chopped
- 3 garlic cloves, crushed
- 1 3/4 C. chopped tomatoes
- 2 tbsps harissa
- 1 cinnamon stick
- 4 C. vegetable stock
- 2 large potatoes, cut into wedges
- 1 lb pumpkin, cut into wedges, skinned and seeded
- 1/2 C. baby corn
- 1/2 C. sugar snap peas
- 1 1/3 C. cherry tomatoes
- 2 tbsps corn flour
- 1/4 C. chopped of fresh mint
- 1/4 C. chopped fresh coriander
- salt & freshly ground black pepper

Directions

- Stir fry your onions for 7 mins with a low level of heat, in some oil, then combine in the stock, garlic, cinnamon, chopped tomatoes, and harissa.
- Get the mix boiling, place a lid on the pot, and let the contents cook for 12 mins.
- Combine in the potatoes and get everything boiling again then place a lid on the pot, and continue to cook everything for 12 more mins, with a low, level of heat.

- Stir the mix then combine in the corn, and pumpkin, place the lid back on the pot and continue cooking everything for 7 more mins.
- Stir the mix again then combine in the cherry tomatoes and peas.
- Let the peas cook for 7 mins.
- Get a bowl, combine: 4 tbsp of water and the corn flour.
- Combine the mix into your stew and get everything boiling.
- Let the mix boil as you stir then add in the coriander and mint.
- Enjoy.

Amount per serving: 6

Timing Information:

| Preparation | 25 mins |
| Total Time | 1 hr 5 mins |

Nutritional Information:

Calories	265.9
Cholesterol	0.0mg
Sodium	49.3mg
Carbohydrates	49.6g
Protein	9.2

* Percent Daily Values are based on a 2,000 calorie diet.

Cranberry Tagine

Ingredients

- 3 tbsps olive oil
- 2 red onions, thickly sliced
- 2 tsps fresh ginger, grated
- 1 lb pumpkin, peeled deseeded and cut into large chunks
- 1 tsp cinnamon
- 1 tsp ground coriander
- 1 tsp ground cumin
- 1 tsp harissa
- 1 tbsp honey
- 2 lbs tomato sauce
- 2 oz. dried cranberries
- 1 (14 oz.) can garbanzo beans, drained

Directions

- Begin to stir fry your onions in 2 tbsp of oil, until browned, then combine in the cranberries, ginger, tomato sauce, pumpkin, honey, and pumpkin spices.
- Stir the mix then get everything boiling.
- Once the mix is boiling, place a lid on the pot, set the heat to low, and continue to cook everything for 25 mins.
- Add in the beans when 15 mins of cooking time is left and ensure the beans are tender and cook everything for 10 more mins.
- Serve the mix with some cooked couscous.
- Enjoy.

Amount per serving: 4

Timing Information:

Preparation	20 mins
Total Time	45 mins

Nutritional Information:

Calories	360.9
Cholesterol	0.0mg
Sodium	1490.9mg
Carbohydrates	59.3g
Protein	9.8

* Percent Daily Values are based on a 2,000 calorie diet.

Mediterranean Lamb Sausage Burgers

Ingredients

- 1 tsp salt
- 1/4 tsp fennel seeds
- 1 tsp ground cumin
- 1/2 tsp ground cinnamon
- 1/2 tsp ground coriander
- 1/4 tsp ground turmeric
- 3 cloves garlic, peeled
- 2 tbsps harissa, or to taste (see Ingredient note)
- 1 tbsp tomato paste
- 1 lb lean ground lamb
- 1 tbsp olive oil

Directions

- Mash your fennel seeds and salt with a grinder then combine the mix with the following in a mortar and pestle: cloves, cumin, garlic cloves, cinnamon, turmeric, and coriander.
- Mash everything until it is smooth then add the mix to a bowl with the tomato paste and harissa.
- Get a 2nd bowl and mix the lamb with the spice mix then place a covering of plastic on the bowl.
- Put the bowl in the fridge for 8 hrs.
- Now shape the lamb into burgers and fry each one for 7 mins each side, in hot olive oil.
- Enjoy.

Amount per serving (4 total)

Timing Information:

Preparation	10 m
Cooking	10 m
Total Time	1 d 20 m

Nutritional Information:

Calories	280 kcal
Fat	19 g
Carbohydrates	6.5g
Protein	19.9 g
Cholesterol	76 mg
Sodium	743 mg

* Percent Daily Values are based on a 2,000 calorie diet.

Carrots, Harissa, Peppers, Chicken, and Sausage Couscous

Ingredients

- 3 tbsp olive oil
- 2 lbs chicken thighs
- 12 oz. Italian sausage
- 1 tbsp diced garlic
- 2 onions, minced
- 2 carrots, julienned
- 1/2 stalk celery, chunked
- 1 rutabaga, parsnip, or turnip, chunked
- 1/2 green bell pepper, julienned
- 1/2 red bell pepper, julienned
- 1 can diced tomatoes
- 1 can garbanzo beans
- 2 C. chicken stock
- 2 tsps thyme
- 1 tsp turmeric
- 1 tsp cayenne pepper
- 1/4 tsp harissa
- 1 bay leaf
- 2 zucchini, cut in half
- 2 C. couscous
- 2 C. chicken stock
- 1/2 C. plain yogurt

Directions

- Brown your chicken thighs all over in olive oil.
- Add in your sausage and cook everything until fully done. Once it has cooled dice the sausage into pieces.

- Now stir fry your garlic and onions until tender and see-through then combine in: stock, bay leaf, carrots, harissa, beans, celery, cayenne, tomatoes, turmeric, rutabaga, thyme, red and green peppers.
- Cook for 2 more mins before adding your chicken and sausage.
- Place a lid on the pan and cook for 35 mins until chicken is fully done.
- Add your zucchini and cook for 7 more mins.
- Meanwhile boil 2 C. of chicken stock then pour it over your couscous in a bowl along with 2 tbsps of olive oil.
- Place a covering on the bowl and let it sit for at least 10 mins.
- When plating the dish first layer couscous then some chicken mix and then some yogurt.
- Enjoy.

Amount per serving (6 total)

Timing Information:

Preparation	Cooking	Total Time
45 m	45 m	1 h 30 m

Nutritional Information:

Calories	934 kcal
Fat	39 g
Carbohydrates	80.5g
Protein	62.2 g
Cholesterol	169 mg
Sodium	601 mg

* Percent Daily Values are based on a 2,000 calorie diet.

Thanks for Reading! Now Let's Try Some **Samosas, Biryani,** and **Moroccan** ....

http://bit.ly/1R3gfGh

To grab this **box set** simply follow the link mentioned above, or tap the book cover.

This will take you to a page where you can simply enter your email address and a PDF version of **the box set** will be emailed to you.

I hope you are ready for some serious **cultural cooking**!

http://bit.ly/1R3gfGh

You will also receive updates on my new books, and various musings about food and cultural cooking.

Also don't forget to like and subscribe on the social networks. I love meeting my readers. Links to all my profiles are below so please click and connect :)

Facebook

Twitter

Google +

Come On...
Let's Be Friends :)

I adore my readers and love connecting with them socially. Please follow the links below so we can connect on Facebook, Twitter, and Google+.

Facebook

Twitter

Google +

I also have a blog that I regularly update for my readers so check it out below.

My Blog

Can I Ask A Favour?

If you found this book interesting, or have otherwise found any benefit in it. Then may I ask that you post a review of it on Amazon? Nothing excites me more than new reviews, especially reviews which suggest new topics for writing. I do read all reviews and I always factor feedback into my newer works.

So if you are willing to take ten minutes to write what you sincerely thought about this book then please visit our Amazon page and post your opinions.

Again thank you!

INTERESTED IN MY OTHER COOKBOOKS?

For more great cookbooks check out my Amazon Author page:

For a complete listing of all my books please see my author page.

Made in the USA
Middletown, DE
28 August 2017